Ready to Pull the Retirement Trigger?

ADVANCE PRAISE

I found *Ready To Pull The Retirement Trigger?* to be an exceptional book that brings real clarity to the complex process of retiring. It is written in an easy-to-understand style and has clear steps to navigating this life-changing event that can be so daunting for many Americans. Mary's personal stories will help readers fully understand the important connection between money and life.

-Valerie G. Brown, Executive Chairman, Advisor Group

In this clear and straightforward gem of a book, readers find valuable information and tools to help allay their fears, discover their choices, and prepare for the retirement experience they desire.

-Rick Fergesen, President, Woodbury Financial

This is a fantastic book for anyone approaching retirement. It takes the complex and explains it in an easy-to-understand manner, providing action steps designed to help readers prepare for a successful retirement.

-Clayton St. George MBA, CLU, CFP®,
Regional Vice President, Woodbury Financial

Mary gets to the heart of the emotions all of us face when we're considering the option of retirement. Not only is she sensitive to the feelings that can hinder sound decision-making, she provides clear steps and strategies for navigating the future.

-Teresa B. Easler, CEO, Connect To The Core Inc.

This book by Mary Sterk is so concrete in its advice for being "Ready To Pull The Retirement Trigger." I think it is one of the clearest and most helpful books available on this subject. As more and more members of our generation reach this decision point, the advice here will be so very helpful. I know it is for me. It also has very helpful ideas for the clients I am advising who are considering retirement.

-Nick Muller, Nicholas G. Muller Law Office, LLC

This book is a great asset for those approaching retirement. It is not too long, and it is written for the reader who is starting at ground zero in retirement planning. It begins by asking all those questions that scare us about choosing to retire. And it provides a blueprint for answering the questions and planning for the future. It does so in clear and understandable terms for the beginner, and provides increasing confidence in your decision-making as you learn how to approach your new life style.

Mary takes the future retiree on a learning journey with Action Steps along the way to summarize and provide an outline for what needs to be done. The complexities of budget-making and estimating future income needs are made simple.

Providing for heirs, managing risk, choosing pension formats, health insurance, nursing home insurance, social security are all topics covered in a way that helps the reader to a new level of security and confidence in their planning. There is even a section on Medicare and how it works, a subject most of us know too little about, but one about which we are afraid to admit our ignorance. It's all there, but it's short, clear and designed to strengthen that shaky retirement trigger. Read this book, and you will be ready to prepare your strategies with confidence in your decisions.

-Francis J. Colella, Ph. D., Economics

An engaging and informative read. Relatable anecdotes help drive home important lessons from money philosophy to planning and portfolio design. Definitely recommended for anyone who hopes for a stress-free retirement—next year or thirty years from now.

-Melanie M. Arnold, CFA, CAIA

Ready To Pull The Retirement Trigger? breaks down the entire retirement process into bite-size pieces that are easy to do. The book provides a clear, concise plan that not only takes the fear and uncertainty out of the retirement process, but frames it in such a way as to make it an enjoyable experience! Even though this is a book about retirement, Sterk's plan is so helpful that it should be required reading for everyone, regardless of age.

-Karrie R. Hruska, Estate Planning Attorney,
Moore Heffernan Law

READY TO PULL THE
RETIREMENT
TRIGGER?

YOUR STRATEGIC GUIDE TO
RETIRE WITH CONFIDENCE

MARY STERK, CFP®

NEW YORK

NASHVILLE • MELBOURNE • VANCOUVER

READY TO PULL THE RETIREMENT TRIGGER?

YOUR STRATEGIC GUIDE TO RETIRE WITH CONFIDENCE

© 2017 Mary Sterk, CFP

Published in New York, New York, by Morgan James Publishing. Morgan James and The Entrepreneurial Publisher are trademarks of Morgan James, LLC.
www.MorganJamesPublishing.com

The Morgan James Speakers Group can bring authors to your live event. For more information or to book an event visit The Morgan James Speakers Group at
www.TheMorganJamesSpeakersGroup.com.

Shelfie

A free eBook edition is available
with the purchase of this print book.

CLEARLY PRINT YOUR NAME ABOVE IN UPPER CASE

Instructions to claim your free eBook edition:
1. Download the Shelfie app for Android or iOS
2. Write your name in **UPPER CASE** above
3. Use the Shelfie app to submit a photo
4. Download your eBook to any device

ISBN 978-1-68350-238-8 paperback
ISBN 978-1-68350-239-5 eBook
Library of Congress Control Number:
2016915391

Cover Design by:
Megan Whitney
megan@creativeninjadesigns.com

Interior Design by:
Chris Treccani
www.3dogdesign.net

In an effort to support local communities, raise awareness and funds, Morgan James
Publishing donates a percentage of all book sales for the life of each book to
Habitat for Humanity Peninsula and Greater Williamsburg.

Get involved today! Visit
www.MorganJamesBuilds.com

DISCLAIMER

Neither the author nor the publisher assumes any responsibility for errors, omissions, or contrary interpretations of the subject matter herein. Any perceived slight of any individual or organization is purely unintentional.

Brand and product names are trademarks or registered trademarks of their respective owners.

Client names, locations, and monetary values have been changed to protect confidentiality.

Any links in this material are provided as a convenience and for informational purposes only. The links are not part of the Woodbury Financial Services, Inc. website, and Woodbury Financial does not endorse or accept any responsibility for the content or use of the website nor guarantee the accuracy or completeness of the data or other information appearing on the linked pages. The company assumes no liability for any inaccuracies, errors, or omissions in or from any data or other information provided on the pages, or for any actions taken in reliance on any such data or information.

DEDICATION

To my children—you were my inspiration to learn about money in the first place, and you are my reason for creating a lasting legacy of love.

TABLE OF CONTENTS

INTRODUCTION

Are you ready to pull the retirement trigger? Talk about a loaded question! You may find yourself thinking, "I want to retire... slow down a bit... enjoy my life, my spouse, and my grandkids."

Then the questions begin to swirl. What if there is a major health issue? Or what if I run out of money? Do I even have enough saved? How much do I really need? Is it invested the best way? What if I have to go into a nursing home? When do I take my Social Security? What do I do with my 401k when I retire? What do I do about health insurance if I retire early?

A few years ago, I worked with a couple who were in their mid-50s, Gelt and Tammy. I happen to be a private pilot, and fly a little Piper Cherokee 235. Gelt was my flight instructor. As he would teach me maneuvers in the plane, we would chit chat about his dream to quit his job managing an

Iowa-based logistics company so he could spend more time doing what he loved–anything to do with airplanes.

When Gelt and Tammy came into the office to create a retirement plan, he thought he would have to work 10 more years before he could retire to pursue this passion. After assessing their situation and what their goals were, I was able to help him create a strategy which would allow retirement within two years instead of 10. The idea of being able to spend his time with aviation-related activity instead of the boring old 9-5 was so exciting for him! And he did it– Gelt quit the job and went to flight mechanic school just for fun. Now, Gelt doesn't have to work because he needs the money, he does it because he loves working on planes. The last several years, he has spent the winters in Texas working on old bomber planes, and the summers in Alaska working on float planes.

Good planning bought Gelt eight years of his life doing exactly what he wanted. Is there a way for you to do the same?

Many people don't know where to find the answers to the retirement questions running through their mind. They also don't know who they can trust to give them good advice. The sheer amount of complexity involved in planning a retirement can be overwhelming. The natural reaction for a lot of people approaching retirement is to stick their head in the sand and avoid the issue altogether! After all, you know what life is like while you are still working, but life after retirement is a big unknown. That can be both scary and exciting!

Here's the thing: there are no do-overs in retirement. Although there are many good ways to set yourself up for success, you can't un-pull the retirement trigger. You only get one shot at this. You need a path. You need a strategy. You need a guide. This book will arm you with the essential knowledge you need to create a strategic plan, so you can retire with confidence.

When can you confidently retire? There is a moment when work becomes optional. This critical point is what I like to call the retirement mecca. Most people see this as an elusive, moving target. The good news is that we can help you figure out what this point is, and how to best get there. Finding your own personal retirement mecca is well within your grasp. When you know the exact point in life when work becomes optional, you have reached the juncture where you can confidently pull the retirement trigger–if you want to.

Yes, I said "if" you want to. The beauty of work being optional is that you can choose to work, or you can choose not to. Inherent in the word "optional" is the concept of choice. When you reach the moment work has become optional, you can choose to continue working–but you don't HAVE to. You can choose to slow down and work part time. Or you can choose to quit the job you've had for 20 years and pursue something that lights the fires of your passion... that thing you've been dreaming about all of these years. The bottom line is this: when work becomes optional, you no longer are a slave to the job or to working in order to have health insurance. It's a delicious level of freedom, and I am going to show you how to find that elusive point so you can confidently make a change when you are ready.

There are three major areas of focus that contribute to a successful retirement: emotional readiness, health-related issues, and financial factors. A high level of retirement confidence comes from having your ducks in a row in all three of these areas. Solving one while ignoring the others is not a good plan. Strategically maximize them all, and your retirement mecca beckons.

The path toward retiring with confidence has a number of steps: 1) understand your own money philosophy; 2) determine what you want your retirement years to feel and be like; 3) address the strengths and weaknesses of where you are right now; 4) create a strategy to bridge the gap from where you are now to the ideal retirement; and 5) pull the retirement trigger!

Sounds easy when you boil it down to just those five steps. But this is where it begins to get complex; each step has nuances and considerations that are unique to you. The ultimate goal in your final strategy is to build upon your strengths, shore up the gaps that can cause problems, and structure things in a way that allows you to protect and grow what you have built. How do you do that? Let's dig in!

Action Steps To Retire With Confidence:

→• Understand your own money philosophy.

→• Determine what you want your retirement years to feel and be like.

→• Assess the strengths and weaknesses of where you are right now.

→• Create a strategy to bridge the gap from where you are now to the ideal retirement.

→• Pull the retirement trigger!

CHAPTER 1

YOUR MONEY PHILOSOPHY

"Darn it! I saved too much for retirement!"
- said nobody, ever

What the heck is a money philosophy? Guess what? You already have a money philosophy–you just may not know it! Simply put, your money philosophy is what you feel money does for you in your life. Sure, money has a monetary value. But it also has a life value, meaning that money funds things that we value in our lives.

Everyone leads a unique life, and we all value different things in our own personal way. You may value the experience of traveling the world, while your next door neighbor values spending time in their garden, nurturing the growth of vegetables and flowers. Perhaps you value a higher university education while your friend values the lessons taught through trade school. Maybe providing a loving home for abused pets matters a lot to you, while your spouse gets excited about programs that support young children. Whatever captures your interest generally takes some level of money to support. How you use the money you have to fund your time, experience, and connection to the things you value IS your money philosophy.

Let me share with you how I developed my money philosophy. It has shaped my life and my financial business, and is ultimately why I chose to write this book.

By the time I was 19 years old, I was already a divorced single mother of two kids under two years old. We lived in a low-rent apartment complex, and I bought my groceries with food stamps. I didn't get any child support and had to desperately try to make ends meet with my minimum wage job and a welfare check.

When I looked around me, I realized that many people in these apartments had been there for years. They were never able to dig themselves out of the financial hole that they were in. I didn't want that to be what my future held. I didn't want to let the fact that I had been a pregnant teenager dictate the rest of my life. I didn't want to be another statistic. I wanted something better for myself and my children. And I realized that in order to create a better life for us, I had to learn how money worked.

So I spent my days working and taking care of my kids, and I spent my nights with my nose in a book, taking classes. This was hard. I was exhausted for about five years. But I learned a number of really important things along the way that have shaped my money philosophy, and ultimately defined how I work with clients today. Here is what I learned.

Money is not about the material things you buy. Sure, it's nice to have quality things, but that's not the main purpose of money. Money is also not about the feelings of happiness or security that many people associate with it. In my opinion, the only thing that money really does is buy you choices. When you have no money, your choices for how to live your life seem very limited. But when you do have money, you can choose to use the money you have to fund the life you want to live.

That's it—that's my money philosophy: money buys you choices. So how does that connect to confidently knowing when to pull the retirement trigger? Here's how. When it comes to retirement planning, any advisor can give you graphs and charts and numbers. Heck, you can even create that yourself on the internet these days if you really want to. But what I am really, really good at is understanding what's most important to you, and then helping you align the money you have with the life that you choose to live. And that is what a good retirement plan is all about.

I have used that very money philosophy to create value for hundreds of clients as I built my financial planning practice. What started as a simple desire to provide a better life for myself and my children has taken me from welfare to wealth management. By studying hard, I was able to obtain my Certified Financial Planner™ certification, and I now lead a large financial planning practice staffed by an amazing team of talented advisors. We are headquartered in South Dakota, with nine affiliated offices across the Midwest that serve clients nationwide.

My passion in life–my purpose, if you will–is to inspire people to create their own best future. If I can show you how to use the money you have to create the life and retirement that you want, then I feel I'm living my purpose. There is truly no better feeling than having a positive impact on someone's life and future.

So how do you really dial into what your money philosophy is? Let me give you three questions to consider that will help you get there.

1. If you had all the money you'll ever need or want, what would you spend time doing?

2. What legacy, if any, would you like to leave? What is important to you about the impact you leave on this world?

3. What was money like for you growing up?

The answers to these questions inform your money philosophy. They tell you what really matters in your life, and that you probably will want to allocate money in your retirement toward those things. What does that mean? Here are some examples.

In question one, if you said you would spend your time traveling the globe, then you might want to build a travel budget into your retirement plan for the first 5-10 years. If you said you want to spend your time painting all day, you might want to include money for art supplies and studio space. Perhaps you want to spend time volunteering at the local soup kitchen. Consider the idea that you may also want to make monetary contributions as you volunteer.

In question two, if you said the impact you want to make is showing your children and grandchildren that spending time with family matters, then you may want to include money in your plan for airfare to visit long-distance family. If you said your legacy is to leave your wisdom for generations to come by writing your memoirs, then perhaps you want to set aside funds to self-publish your book. Perhaps you want to provide a college education for great-grandchildren–then you may consider isolating a chunk of your retirement assets for that specific goal, or consider funding that legacy through a life insurance program.

The first two questions also help assess your emotional readiness as you contemplate retirement. Many people are unsure about how they will spend their time once they stop working. They question how to stay mentally sharp and socially engaged. People tend to feel more confident of their next step when they have given thought to how they will remain active and contributing members of their community. These questions open the door to dream about how you might spend your future time in a way that feels purposeful, productive and peaceful. The more narrowly you hone in on this, the more emotionally ready you will be to pull the retirement trigger.

What does question three indicate? There is a strong link between the lessons we learned about money as we grew up, and the way we feel about money right now. If you grew up feeling like money was no big deal and there was plenty to go around, you are more likely to feel comfortable with higher levels of risk. You most likely don't lose much sleep worrying about having enough cash. You would probably prefer a strategy with a bit more emphasis on growth potential vs. protecting against loss at any cost.

However, if you grew up where money was tight or even nonexistent, you are more likely to worry about there being a scarcity of money later in life. It can be difficult to feel safe or secure, even if you know there's money in the bank. You are likely to be more concerned about not losing money vs. actually growing it. Your strategy would probably require more emphasis on protecting value, as opposed to growing at high rates.

Of course, not everyone fits perfectly into one of these "types," but generally speaking, you probably can recognize yourself in one of these viewpoints. It is important to know this, because it speaks directly to how much risk you should blend into your retirement portfolio.

You may have heard the term "risk tolerance" and are wondering what that really means. Simply put, risk tolerance means how much fluctuation you can stomach in your own accounts as markets move up and down. There is no right or wrong with risk tolerance. It all just comes down to how you feel. If you can handle the ups and downs without losing a wink of sleep, then you have a more aggressive level of risk tolerance. If the value of your account dropping–even just a bit–makes your stomach churn, then you have a more conservative risk tolerance. Oftentimes, people land somewhere in the middle of these extremes, and we call that a moderate risk tolerance.

Over time, your tolerance for risk is likely to shift. As you get closer to pulling the retirement trigger, you may find yourself moving from aggressive toward more moderate. Or from moderate toward conservative. Everyone is different, but what's important is that you determine what your own level is.

So how do you know what your risk tolerance is? Fortunately, that's really easy! There are dozens of short quizzes that you can find on the internet or through your financial advisor to really zero in on your personal risk tolerance level. We have assembled a Strategic Retirement Tool Kit* that you can download for free from our website. It includes a number of tools that we'll talk about in this book, and among them is a Risk Tolerance Quiz. It has a few questions and a simple scoring system that will help you determine how much risk you're comfortable with. Maybe a little, maybe a lot–who knows? The important thing is that you determine your risk tolerance level, as it is an important piece of your money philosophy.

A good retirement plan will align the money you have with the life you want to live. It will fund the experiences and activities that matter to you. A strong strategy will connect the value of your money to the people and things in life that you value. It will also identify exactly how much risk you personally

---

*   http://www.sterkfinancialservices.com/p/toolkit

feel comfortable with in your retirement portfolio. Therein lies your own personal money philosophy, which is the foundation of your retirement planning.

Action Steps To Determine Your Money Philosophy:

→• Answer the three questions.

→• Determine how much money you will want to use each year to fund the things, people, and experiences you value.

→• Take the Risk Tolerance Quiz and find your personal risk level.

CHAPTER 2

LOOKING AHEAD

"I wish my wallet came with free refills!"

Retirement has been called the Golden Years, the Eternal Saturday, and the Final Chapter. Personally I don't think any of those labels apply anymore. The retirement your grandfather desired probably consisted mostly of sitting on the front porch in his rocking chair, watching the world go by. While you are likely looking forward to time spent relaxing, the retirements of today are dramatically different and usually much more active than the retirements of yesteryear.

In fact, many people simply have no idea how they will actually spend their time when they stop working. The questions begin to swirl again. What if I'm bored? What will I spend time doing? What if my spouse gets sick of me hanging around the house? Once I get my list of projects done, what will I do next? What if I end up wishing I hadn't quit my job? Can I afford to do the things I actually want to do?

Let me share Helen's story with you. Helen spent her career as a distinguished college professor in the upper Midwest, teaching art history to young talented minds. Her love of both the old masters and contemporary artists created a learning environment for her students that inspired amazing work. She had spent time during her academic years creating her own art, but it was always sandwiched in when time allowed between her teaching job and raising a family.

When Helen was contemplating retirement, we spent time visiting about what really mattered to her. She discovered that she had a dual desire: to create beauty in the world, and to help the less fortunate living in third-world countries. Helen had saved around $500,000 in retirement accounts, and I was able to help her design a strategy to include funding for both desires in her retirement plan. We allotted a set amount for studio space, gallery and show fees, and painting supplies, so she could create new art to brighten the world. We also included funds designated for charitable giving and travel expenses in her annual budget during the first five years of her retirement, so Helen could contribute to helping those in need.

The time Helen took to dream ahead about how she wanted retirement to look and feel made all the difference. She solidified her emotional readiness by carefully considering what mattered most, and allocating resources to it. So here is your chance. What do you really want? I invite you to envision your future without judgement. This is not the time to worry about the "how"–we will flesh that out later. If your dream is to retire and open a bakery in Paris, don't worry about the details of the work visa, focus on the taste of the chocolate pastry! I don't know if you'll be able to align your money with fulfilling every one of your dreams, but I do know that in order to try, we have to understand what those dreams are made of.

Next, we begin to connect the emotional readiness with the financial data. By developing your own personal Money Philosophy in chapter 2 and with the work we'll cover in chapter 3, you'll be able to use that information to build the framework for your financial needs during retirement. For this step, you'll need to take a look backwards at how you have been spending money, and then look ahead at what you will be spending money on in the future.

Some of you reading this might be starting to cringe as you anticipate the dreaded B-word. Believe me, I fully recognize that no one likes the word "budget"! In fact, some of you may want to put down this book and stop reading altogether. But don't! I'm not suggesting that you need to live on a budget, or that you have to follow an exact budget once you pull the retirement trigger. Let me show you how a budget plays into your planning without making it too complex.

There are two ways to create a framework for determining the moment when work becomes optional. The first way is to estimate your needs. The second way is to use a budget tool to lay out a more precise cash flow plan.

If you want a rough estimate, use your tax return as a guide. Take your gross income and subtract your federal and state taxes, your FICA taxes, and your retirement plan contributions. This will give you an approximate idea of the amount of money you're currently living on. The upside of estimating is that it gets you a number quickly and easily. The downside is that estimating really only shows you how you've been living in the past, not how you plan to live going forward.

If you want a more definitive number, use a budget tool as a guide. First, find a budget tool that you feel comfortable with. Some self-proclaimed math nerds like me opt to use Excel spreadsheets. Others prefer a paper ledger. We have created a fantastic Budget Tool as part of our Strategic Retirement Tool Kit* that you can download for free. Word of warning: not all budget tools are created equal. There are certain things a strong budget tool should include:

1. The budget tool should show a monthly as well as a yearly view. Expenses like property taxes may only happen twice a year. If your budget tool is only a one-month look, you're likely to miss some things that don't occur each and every month.

2. The budget tool should have space for incomes and space for expenses. A strong tool will have formulas built in to show where you have gaps between income and expenses once you've entered your information.

3. The budget tool should suggest categories for you, including ones that are easy to forget. Do you spend extra in December for Christmas gifts? What about lawn services in the summer and snow blowing in the winter? Did you include getting your hair done every two months?

4. The budget tool should clearly note which expenses are fixed—meaning they don't really change much month

---

* http://www.sterkfinancialservices.com/p/toolkit

to month or year to year. You also should be able to easily see which expenses are variable–meaning they are likely to shift and change over time.

5. The budget tool should give you a place to note your future incomes as well as your future expenses. This will make the creation of your final retirement strategy much simpler in later steps.

Once you have settled on the right budget tool, pull together all the information on what you have been spending. Gather your checkbook, your bank statements, and your debit and credit card histories for the last three months. Use this information to fill in the expenses section of your budget tool. At this point, don't worry about the income side–that will come later. For now, we're only concerned with learning what you have been spending and what cash needs you are likely to have during your initial retirement years.

First, go through the statements you've gathered and plug in the relevant numbers to get an idea of what you are actually spending money on right now. Then think through the rest of the year to bring in the items and experiences you spend money on that are occasional, rather than monthly expenses. Enter those things into your budget tool.

Next, consider the fact that certain expenses you currently have may not continue once you are retired. You may spend less in gas if you are no longer commuting. Perhaps your clothing budget will shift if you no longer need as many suits and ties. Make adjustments to your budget tool to reflect what you are likely to spend in the future.

Finally, go back to your money philosophy questions. Add into your budget tool the money you would like to have to support the things, people, and experiences you value. What you will have created is the financial framework for your early years of retirement.

There are several things to make note of at this point. First, there is an insidious little retirement devil called inflation that we must address. Inflation just means that over time, it will cost more each year to live the exact same lifestyle. No one actually knows what inflation will be in the future, but we can look at the past as a guide. In the last 10 years, inflation has been fairly low, averaging just under two percent. However, if we look at a broader time period, we see longer term trends of inflation closer to four percent with occasional spikes over 10 percent.

So why does this matter? Because inflation impacts your ability to stretch a dollar. We call this purchasing power. The higher the inflation, the less a dollar buys. Inflation can make it look like you need a crazy high amount of money when you are in your 90s just to live on. But think about it: your grandfather would have never believed that someday he'd pay $4 for a gallon of milk, when at one time he could buy that for a dime! In your retirement planning, you start with figuring out your current needs, but eventually, you will have to bring potential inflation increases into the picture. If you don't, you're setting yourself up to lose purchasing power.

Counter-balancing the negative impact of inflation is the reality that as you age, you tend to spend less. Most people travel the most during the first five to 10 years of retirement. This is also when people tend to spend more money on clothes, vehicles, gas, and entertainment. While your medical costs may go up over time, there are quite a number of expenses that will actually go down as you age. In fact, according to a recent Consumer Expenditure Survey, people age 75+ spend 40 percent less than people who are 55-64, and 26 percent less than those who are 65-74.

Some of the above are big expenses, but chances are, you won't make them every year. Perhaps you buy a car every five years. Maybe you take a cruise every other summer. Are you planning a trip to Disney with the grandkids three years from now? If you already know about big-ticket future expenses, make a note of them at the bottom of your budget tool so you don't forget that they're part of your plan.

Inflation and changing needs are complex financial issues that can derail retirement planning. People frequently are at a loss when it comes to calculating inflation and using it as a meaningful factor in their plan. They struggle to account for non-linear future spending. Many times, people throw their hands in despair, thinking, "I can never retire!" Fortunately, there are great tools available to help you grasp what your future financial needs might be.

We will bring inflation, your decreasing pattern of spending as you age, and your occasional future spending needs into the picture again when it's time to create your final strategy. For now, just remember that as you look forward, your purchasing power and spending patterns will fluctuate over your lifetime. A good plan will take that into consideration.

I know this step can seem boring and tedious. But you can't pinpoint the moment when work becomes optional until you look ahead and determine your future cash needs. Once you have completed this step, you will have the financial framework built for initial cash outflow during your retirement. This is a critical piece of information that helps draw a connection between your emotional readiness and the financial components. This step draws a line that connects how you want your retirement to look and feel to how much money you need to support that vision.

Action Steps To Determine How You Want Retirement To Look And Feel:

→• Decide if you will estimate or use a budget tool.

→• If you estimate, calculate your current net spending number.

→• If you wish to be more exact, find a strong budget tool.

→• Gather your information about past spending.

→• Fill in the expenses section of your budget framework with past spending data and occasional expense information, and allocate dollars to support your Money Philosophy desires.

→• Project inflation, reduced spending as you age, and non-annual expenses.

CHAPTER 3

WHERE ARE YOU NOW?

"I'm going to retire and live off my savings. What I'll do the second week I have no idea!"

- Aunty Acid

A wise business coach once told me that all progress starts by telling the truth of where you are right now. If you want to progress toward retiring with confidence, then you have to get very clear on where you are right now and how that impacts your future.

Clarity comes from knowing what you currently have in place, understanding your strengths, and becoming aware of your weaknesses. The type of clarity a strong retirement plan includes can be broken down into four areas: health, money, legacy, and risk.

First, you must gather some data. People are often unsure of which specific information is important, so we have built a handy list. You can find this List of Confidential Documents within our downloadable Strategic Retirement Tool Kit[*]. The primary information you will want to have handy includes:

- ☐ Any legal paperwork you have created: will, trust, power of attorney documents, etc.
- ☐ A copy of your recent tax return
- ☐ Information on what the following insurance policies cover:
  - o Auto
  - o Home
  - o Umbrella
  - o Health
  - o Life
  - o Disability
  - o Long-Term Care
  - o Group Benefits
- ☐ Your Social Security projections

---

*   http://www.sterkfinancialservices.com/p/toolkit

☐ Data on expected payouts from pensions

☐ Full statements on investment accounts, 401(k)s, IRAs, CDs, annuities, stocks, etc.

☐ Current figures on debt and the interest rate it carries

☐ Bank statements showing checking, savings, or money market balances

☐ Estimates of value for your property like home, farm, rentals, business, etc.

Once you have gathered this information, you can begin to flush out your strengths and weaknesses in each of the four major categories–health, money, legacy, and risk. Both the health and money categories are where most people's key fears and uncertainties lie, so I will spend an entire chapter on each of those. The legacy and risk areas are equally important within a strong retirement plan, so I also want to have some discussion on each of those.

Leaving A Legacy

Your legacy can mean a number of things. It can be the personal impact you made on people or on the earth itself. Or it might mean a financial impact you leave on family or charity. When we were talking about developing your Money Philosophy, I posed a question about leaving a legacy. This should have gotten you started thinking about this. I want to educate you on three things that impact the way your financial legacy gets carried out: beneficiary designations, estate-planning documents, and trusts.

First, let's address beneficiary designations. I have seen many occasions where someone has forgotten to change their beneficiary after a major life change. This has resulted in money being left to an ex-spouse instead of a current one, or later-born grandchildren getting left out of the inheritance! My recommendation is that you take time to review the beneficiary listings on every single account or pension that you have. A primary beneficiary is who gets the money if you die. A contingent beneficiary is who gets the money if both you and all of your primary beneficiaries are dead. Make sure your wishes are reflected in the listings on your accounts!

Next, let's talk about estate-planning documents. At the very least, I believe everyone should have a three-pack of legal documents that includes a Will, a Financial Power of Attorney, and a Health Care Power of Attorney.

The Will determines who gets your stuff. If you don't have one, the state you live in will decide who gets it, and that may not be how you want things to roll. Married or single, you should still have a Will.

The Financial Power of Attorney is a standby document, which means it doesn't actually take effect until such time as you are mentally unable to handle your own affairs. When and if that happens, it gives someone you trust the power to deal with your financial accounts on your behalf.

The Health Care Power of Attorney is a bit broader than a Living Will. It does cover your wish to pull the plug or not pull the plug, but it also acts as a standby document to give someone you trust the ability to make health care decisions for you if you are unable to do so yourself. It is expensive to have a person appointed as a Power of Attorney when you need help, and much less expensive to take care of that ahead of time with good documents.

Many people also wonder about trusts as a way to handle their legacy. There are many types of trusts, and this arena can be quite complex. Here is a simple overview about three types of trusts that are commonly used in estate planning.

Trusts Made Simple

A **Testamentary Trust** is created by your will when you die. Beyond writing it into your will, you don't have to set it up ahead of time or fund it while you are alive. This is typically used to handle the flow of money over time for minor children or grandchildren, or to help in a situation where a child might be financially irresponsible. In your will, you create the trust's rules, which explain how the money and property will be handled once you are gone. You also name a trustee in the will–someone who you feel confident will honor your wishes and abide by the rules of the trust. Assets that flow into a Testamentary Trust through your will go through the court system in a process called probate. Probate has associated costs that can frequently reach 2-4% of the estate value. Whatever goes through the probate court is a matter of public record. Once it has gone through probate, the assets are then titled into the Testamentary Trust and the trustee begins to oversee everything on behalf of your heirs.

A **Revocable Living Trust** means you set it up and fund it while you are alive. You can also change it while you are alive. It acts like your alter ego, using the same tax ID number as yours. The trust document spells out the rules and the trustee responsibilities that will come into effect once you have passed away. This type of trust is typically used to avoid many of the costs of probate, and to handle the flow of money and property over time. Revocable Living Trusts also keep your affairs private, so no one can snoop into your business through the court systems once you have passed away.

Let me give you an example of when a Revocable Living Trust is a good idea. I have three children ages 25, 22, and 17. I also have one grandson (love of my life!) who is four. I have a personal belief that large sums of money left to young adults is a recipe for trouble. So I created a Revocable Living Trust and moved all of my property and investments inside of it. When I die, there will be money to take care of my children's needs and education only. If my grandson's mama is no longer living, then there are provisions for using the money to take care of him as he grows up. When my darling kiddos reach the age of 25, they will receive a third of their inheritance.

I love my kids, but I am pretty sure they will blow the first chunk. I have seen this happen time and time again when younger people inherit large sums of money. Unfortunately, it is a fairly common issue. Fortunately, using a trust in a smart way can alleviate the potential of them blowing ALL of it! That's why they only get a third. They will get another third when they are 30. I hope they remember the lessons they learned from blowing the first chunk! I hope they are smart enough to use the money for something important like a house, a business purchase, or to fund their own children's education. My kids will receive their final third when they are 35. If they haven't learned any money lessons by this time, then I give up! But I hope that by this age they have matured enough to make wise financial decisions that will create a lasting impact in their lives and the future generations to come.

An **Irrevocable Trust** is completely different from the first two types we have discussed. You set up an Irrevocable Trust and fund it while you are alive, but you cannot change it in the future. It is frequently used to hold life insurance for estate planning and tax reduction purposes. Irrevocable Trusts can also be used to handle a family issue such as funds for a special needs child. Once you put assets into this trust, you lose control of the asset and there is no flexibility on this. Because of the lack of flexibility, it is not a tool that is used in most estates. However, large tax situations created by significant wealth may greatly benefit by utilizing an Irrevocable Trust.

Not having any estate planning documents is an obvious weakness. It also may be a weak area if your documents were written a long time ago–especially if your life has changed dramatically since then. Something as simple as becoming a grandparent often necessitates a revision of your will. I suggest that as you enter retirement, you seek an attorney you feel comfortable with to draw up the documents that will manage your legacy in the way you desire.

The bottom line is this: inheriting money frequently creates a new dynamic within families that is not always pretty. Unfortunately, it can create squabbles between siblings and a poor work ethic in young people. It is difficult to predict exactly how someone will react to a large inflow of money. I encourage you to spend some time considering the personalities of your beneficiaries, and to set up your estate-planning documents to provide for a best possible outcome. You have spent time and effort accumulating your wealth, so make sure you put some time and effort into planning for the impact you want your legacy to create. Strengthen your retirement planning by creating or revising documents and beneficiary designations that align with the lasting legacy you wish to leave.

Managing Your Risk

There will always be risks in life. Some we can choose to insure against. This section will discuss some key risks you need to focus on while planning for your retirement.

Everyone needs car and home insurance. If your net worth is over $1,000,000, you should consider layering on an umbrella policy. An umbrella policy is designed to add liability protection on top of what your home or auto policy provides. Let me give you an example:

A number of years ago, I worked with some clients who had just pulled the retirement trigger. Hank and Elsa were in their early 60s and had a beautiful home with a lovely pool. They frequently enjoyed hosting dinner parties on their patio. One evening, tragedy struck. A guest was accidentally bumped into the pool. She landed in such a way that broke her neck, and she was paralyzed for the rest of her life. The injured guest's medical bills ran into the millions.

Fortunately, Hank and Elsa had the foresight to add an umbrella policy prior to retiring. Their homeowners' insurance paid out its max of $500,000, and then their umbrella policy allowed them to pay out $1,000,000 more. Having the policy in place prevented their sizable retirement assets from getting eaten up by a lawsuit due to this terrible accident. Talk to your insurance agent to determine what the right limits are to protect you in your auto, home, and umbrella coverage.

Another hot topic in retirement planning is life insurance. You may be wondering things like: Do I still need life insurance? What is the right type? How much coverage should I have?

I like to think that there are three distinct roles that life insurance plays during our lifetimes. When we are young, life insurance is there to protect our spouses and children if we die too soon. During middle age, life insurance is used to ensure your spouse has a comfortable financial situation if you pass away early on in your retirement. Once we have made it to a ripe old age, the purpose of life insurance shifts once again. At that point, the role of life insurance is to create a financial legacy for your family or for charity.

The time to evaluate your future life insurance needs is *before* you pull the retirement trigger. You have to look at how your spouse would survive if you do not. They would lose a Social Security check. They may lose a pension. Life insurance can be a good way to back-fill this potential income gap. Permanent life insurance policies can shape shift over time—starting out as retirement protection and later becoming used for legacy goals. You should know the costs of life insurance that you expect to incur during retirement so you can include them in your budget tool.

There are a wide variety of types and styles of life insurance, which is a much bigger topic in scope than I can cover in this book. Take time to understand the coverages that you have in place. Visit with your financial advisor about the exact right amount of insurance you need to cover the goals that you have. You may find that you have too much coverage, which can free up some expenses during retirement. Conversely, you may find that you need to add some life insurance, and can evaluate with your advisor the right type and amount to add.

The last insurance that I want to mention is disability insurance. I am a big believer in carrying disability insurance during your working years. Why? Because your biggest asset is actually your ability to earn income. That being said, once you pull the retirement trigger there is no more income generation happening that requires protection. Many people don't realize that if you become disabled during a period when you don't actually have a job, your policy won't pay a benefit. In my opinion, there is no reason to keep a disability policy beyond the point in time when you actually retire.

Gaps in your overall insurance planning create a level of risk that is a weakness in your retirement planning. We have created a worksheet in our Strategic Retirement Tool Kit* that helps you ask key questions to determine if you have significant insurance gaps. Mitigate your risk by reviewing your existing coverages and making sure you have adequate limits. Shore up your planning by reviewing the phase of life insurance that you are in, and aligning your coverage amounts with your retirement goals.

---

*   http://www.sterkfinancialservices.com/p/toolkit

Action Steps For Gaining Clarity on Legacy and Risk Planning:

→• Gather your important data together to evaluate strengths and weaknesses.

→• Update your beneficiaries.

→• Get your three-pack of estate-planning documents created or revised.

→• Cover your backside! Make sure you have high enough limits of auto, home, and umbrella coverage.

→• Determine how much life insurance you need for retirement and legacy goals. Work with your advisor to align your coverage with this need.

CHAPTER 4

THE HEALTHY TRUTH

"All I want for Christmas is one really good bowel movement!"

- Health Callings

Let's talk all things health-related. If you are like most people, the possible health issues that could crop up during retirement are a major concern. What if I get cancer and my health insurance doesn't cover it all? What if I need to go into a nursing home when I am older? How do I handle health insurance if I retire early and can't get Medicare yet? When am I supposed to get set up on Medicare? How much will it all cost?

Recently, I met with Sam and Louise. He is 58 and Louise is 55, and they live in a comfortable suburb in northern

Texas. They have both worked at their jobs for over 20 years. Saving money wasn't always easy, but they made it a priority and accumulated a nice pool of retirement money–over $3 million dollars. They had a mortgage, but no other debt. Sam handled most of the money along the way. Louise knew they had money, but never wanted to manage investments or ever really dig into understanding them too much. They were not looking to live an extravagant lifestyle during retirement, but they wanted to feel comfortable and secure that they would not run out of money. Sam was pretty sure they could retire early–maybe even in a couple of years. Louise's big fear about retiring early was wondering if they would be able to afford health insurance to carry them from an early retirement to Medicare age. Her comment was, "It might cost $1,000 a month for health insurance and I just don't know if we can afford that. If I just work a few extra years, then we won't have to worry about that so much."

If you have considered retiring early, then I bet that sounds familiar! Here's the thing–do you really want to trade years of your life in exchange for health insurance? Or would you rather figure out if you CAN afford it and then decide if you WANT to? Personally, I always opt to make an informed choice rather than a choice driven primarily by fear or uncertainty.

Health Insurance

So here is the current skinny on health insurance. If you worked for a company that had group health insurance, you may be able to extend your coverage with the group for up to 18 months. The length of time you can extend depends on the size of your employer and the group plan State Continuation or Cobra rules. Ask your employer's benefits person what the rules are for your plan, and what the costs are. Then you will know if continuing group coverage can play a part in your early retirement plan.

When you come off of group coverage, you have to replace it with individual coverage. Currently, that's the law. In the days before the Affordable Care Act (seriously, I think they should rename it the *Un*Affordable Care Act!), you could only get individual coverage if you were in great health. Under current law, you can get individual coverage no matter what your health conditions are. It might not be as good of coverage as what you had before. It might be more expensive than what you had before. But it's available to anyone with any health condition. You just have to be able to pay for it.

This change created an amazing bridge for people, giving them the opportunity to plug the health insurance gap between early retirement and Medicare. Although the gap can be plugged, the cost to do so may be quite high. In my example above, Louise was right on the money about the potential cost. You may spend $1,000 a month for coverage. It could be less, it could be more. For you to get clarity about the possible expense to use in your planning, I suggest you visit with a local health insurance agent, or do some online quoting through an Insurance Exchange. Then you will know if individual coverage will be a reasonable option for you.

Both extended group coverage and individual coverage have deductible and upper limits of cost called "out-of-pocket maximums" that you may be responsible for in the event of a health crisis. Take some time to understand what your worst case out-of-pocket maximum might be. If you are not sure, talk to your employee benefits person, your insurance agent, or the company itself. Smart retirees will set aside emergency money to cover this potential expense in order to feel confident that a health issue will not derail their retirement plan.

Medicare

There are a lot of rules within the Medicare system, and for a complete overview of the program, I recommend you check out the website Medicare.gov. While I'm not going to get into the nitty gritty details of all things Medicare, I do want to hit the highlights (note: pricing estimates are current as of 2016).

Medicare Part A – most everyone signs up when they are 65, whether they intend to use it right away or not. It becomes secondary to your employer group coverage if you are still working. It becomes primary coverage if you are not. It mainly covers hospital expenses. There is no cost for it.

Medicare Part B - you sign up at age 65 or when you come off of your employer group coverage–whichever is later. It becomes primary coverage when you take it. It mainly covers doctor expenses. The cost for it runs around $150 a month. You can opt to have it deducted from your Social Security check, or you can pay for it directly.

Medicare Part C - you sign up at age 65 or when you come off of your employer group coverage–whichever is later. It is also called Medicare Advantage. This coverage is a private version of Medicare that combines Part A and Part B benefits and is approved by the government. It may include additional benefits like vision and dental, and frequently requires you see a doctor who is in a specific network. Note that if you elect this coverage, you still have to pay for Part B premiums. The Medicare Advantage coverage is not as widely used as a Part A and Part B combo.

Medicare Part D - you sign up at age 65 or when you come off of your employer group coverage—whichever is later. It covers drugs. The cost for it can run between $5 and $500 a month, and the price is totally dependent upon which drugs you take. There are several levels of plan coverage, and you buy this through an insurance company. If your drug needs change during the year, then in late fall, during a special open enrollment period, you can upgrade or change your plan coverage as needed. Beware the fact that if you don't sign up for it when you are supposed to, there is a monthly penalty that accrues and you will pay that for the rest of your life. That can be a big deal, so you don't want to miss getting this into place.

Medicare Supplement - you sign up at age 65 or when you come off of your employer group coverage—whichever is later. It is designed to cover what Medicare Part A and Part B do not. The cost generally runs around $150 a month for the most popular plan, Plan F. There are a number of coverage options, and you buy this through an insurance company. The interesting thing to note here, though, is that all plan coverages from company to company are identical. Company A's Plan F is the exact same coverage as Company B's Plan F. They will, however, have different pricing, and may have added in some bells and whistles that you find valuable. It's a good idea to talk to a local insurance agent to find out what your supplement options are so you can make an informed choice on plan level and company selection.

Medicare can be confusing and hard to navigate, but in its essence, it boils down to the above pieces. You need Part A, Part B, (or part C), Part D, and a Supplement. Part A and B are done through the government, and Part C, D, and the Supplement are done through a private company that you choose. Make sure to plug the monthly costs of your health insurance needs into your budget tool so you have an accurate picture of the cost when you retire.

Long-term Care

Lastly, let's visit about the biggest health-related fear of them all: the dreaded nursing home. Ugh—no one actually ever wants to go to a nursing home. And you certainly don't want all of your hard-earned money to get eaten up by the high cost of nursing home care. This particular subject is an easy one to get overwhelmed by. Between the fear of you or your spouse ever having to need long-term care, emotion surrounding your own parents' experience, and the sheer complexity of the subject, it's easy to want to stick your head in the sand! So how do you handle this? Let's break it down into simple pieces and address them one at a time.

First, let's talk housing options. Generally speaking, people want to stay in their own homes as long as possible. If you have a health issue that requires significant care, home health care can be a wonderful solution. But while staying in your home is an ideal option, it can often be costly to do so, and take a physical toll on a caregiving spouse. Care at home sometimes requires specialized equipment and remodeling costs to accommodate your needs. Even with that, I think it's fair to say that remaining independent in our own homes is generally our first choice. At some point, though, you have to begin to consider other options.

Transitioning away from your home can happen in several phases. Many people first transition from the home they have lived in for years to an independent living arrangement in a retirement community. Independent living combines the freedom of living in your own structure and on your own terms, with closeness of proximity and access to a larger community of likeminded people.

The next stage is that at some point, you may transition to an assisted living scenario. This means that you are still fairly independent and have your own living quarters, but also have nursing care available as needed or for specific things. This type of arrangement can be good for married couples, because you still can live together and help each other as needed, but know that help is available for some of the more difficult things like help with lifting and bathing, and medication management. Assisted living units are typically connected to a larger building or facility for ease of access to meals, activities, and medical help.

Another transition stage is moving into full-blown nursing home care in which you receive round-the-clock care. You may have a private room, or share a room with another person who needs similar care. At this point, many people have significant health issues and need skilled nursing care for basic needs such as bathing, eating, and dressing. Skilled care often becomes necessary when it has become physically impossible for a spouse to provide the level of care needed. This is a tough transition. Most people resist moving into this stage for as long as possible.

For many people, nursing home care is their last living arrangement. But for some, a final transition occurs if you are challenged with Alzheimer's Disease or dementia. This means moving into a Memory Care unit. Memory Care is usually a locked ward for its residents' protection. It provides a safe and caring environment for people who need the extra level of care associated with loss of mental capacity. Many of us have loved someone who went through this experience. This transition can be devastating, but it's also necessary to provide safe and secure care for people at this stage.

The journey through these stages is a sobering one, and not something most of us care to think about until we have to. The problem lies with the fact that the costs of care later in life can destroy even the most carefully planned retirement. This is especially significant if you are married and one spouse needs expensive care, leaving the other spouse with a deeply slashed budget on which to survive.

So who should protect against this risk, and how do you accomplish this? It is my belief that everyone should consider Long-term Care Insurance, but there are some parameters of when it makes the most sense to actually purchase.

If you have less than $300,000 in retirement assets, the pure expense of Long-term Care Insurance may use up a large percentage of your savings. The cost of insurance can be high—anywhere from $2-5k a year. If you have a smaller amount of retirement assets, it may not be wise to spend such a large chunk annually on insurance. That being said, if your goal is to protect your spouse from a lowered standard of living, preserve your choice of where to stay in a nursing home, or protect assets for your beneficiary, then by all means, insure yourself against this risk.

Conversely, if you have more than $3 million dollars in retirement assets, you should consider the fact that you may have enough assets to self-fund a stay in a care facility. If you can comfortably pull $50,000-70,000 a year from your pool of assets without radically affecting your spouse's standard of living, then long-term care insurance may not be necessary. However, if that is not how you want to CHOOSE to spend your money, then a good insurance policy can protect those hard-earned assets.

It's the people in the middle, with retirement savings between $300k and $3M, who I believe will benefit the most from evaluating the addition of Long-term Care Insurance to their retirement strategy. Let me explain why.

Long-term Care Insurance for single people is not just about preserving assets, but also about quality of care and choice in where they want to live as they transition through the stages of care. Long-term Care Insurance for married people is more about protecting your spouse and preserving assets.

Either you will pay for your nursing home care, or you may be eligible for the state to cover the cost. If you want the state to pay for your nursing home stay, there are some rules. Each state is different, so let me use Iowa as an example. In order to trigger the state to pay for your care, you need to be eligible for Medicaid. In order to be eligible for Medicaid, there are different rules, depending on whether you're single or married.

If you are single, you have to sell your property and spend all of your assets down to roughly $2,000. That means sell your house, your farm, your business–everything. Then you will be eligible to trigger Medicaid, and the state will pay for your nursing home care. It is important to note that not all facilities accept Medicaid patients, so your choices of where to live may be limited.

If you are married, you have to sell everything except your house, and spend down your assets to roughly $80,000. Then you can trigger Medicaid as well. The biggest issue about this is that you'll be leaving your spouse to try to manage the rest of their retirement on only $80,000. In addition, your spouse has been used to receiving your Social Security, pension, or other income. Now, that will all go to the nursing home in order to minimize the state's cost of care.

I am frequently asked if there are ways to beat the system– can't you just give away your property to your kids and plan for the state to take care of you? This is easier said than done. Each state is different, but most have a "Look Back Period" of five years. That means that if you have given away property or money in the past five years before becoming eligible for Medicaid, then you will have a period of ineligibility, or they will claw the property back from the person you gave it to. 29 states also have laws that say an adult child can be held responsible for the elder care of an indigent parent who's ineligible for Medicaid. If this is your plan to protect your assets, then be careful. Consult an elder care attorney in your state to know what you can and can't do within the scope of the law.

So your choices seem to be either spend down your assets (which could leave your spouse in a financial pickle), or insure against the risk (which can be expensive). This feels like a no-win situation. You can see why no one really wants to deal with it. I suggest you pick the lesser of the two evils for your particular situation and move forward.

If you decide to protect retirement income and the value of your assets by getting Long-term Care Insurance, you open up a whole new can of worms–namely, how to understand Long-term Care Insurance itself. Long-term Care Insurance is complex, has a lot of options and moving parts, and can be expensive. I could write an entire book about this topic, but that would bore most of you to tears! For our purposes here, I just want to hit the highlights.

Features of most Long-term Care Insurance policies:

An **elimination period**, typically 90 days, is the amount of time you have to pay for your care before the insurance kicks in. A **daily or monthly benefit** is the amount of money the policy will pay for your care. An **inflation protection or cost of living rider** will increase your daily or monthly benefit by a certain percentage each year to keep your policy benefits in line with the increased cost of care as you age. A **benefit period** will be the length of time your policy will pay out once you start receiving benefits. A **state partnership program** typically allows your family or spouse to preserve assets (equal to the amount of coverage you purchased), and still let you trigger Medicaid eligibility. Note that each state is different, so you will want to do some research on what partnership rules may apply to you.

All Long-term Care Insurance policies have triggers that allow you to go "on claim", meaning that your policy will begin paying benefits. Most policies utilize a standard set of triggers called **Activities of Daily Living**. If you are unable to perform two out of the six following activities, generally you can claim benefits from your policy. The Activities of Daily Living include: bathing, continence, dressing, self-feeding, toileting, and transferring (moving from bed to bathroom). The single trigger of mental incapacity can also allow you to begin claims on your policy.

Comparison of policy types:

There are two main types of Long-term Care policies I would like to address. The type built on a health insurance chassis is called Traditional Coverage. The type built on a life insurance chassis is called Hybrid Coverage. Both have pros and cons and I will highlight a few of them below. (Note: all policies are unique, and care should be taken to investigate all of these points prior to making any type of purchase.)

Traditional Coverage	Hybrid Coverage
Pros:	**Cons:**
Starts out a lower cost	Starts out a higher cost
Usually includes inflation protection	Some do not include inflation protection
May participate in the state partnership	Does not meet partnership criteria
May be tax deductible	Generally not considered tax deductible
Cons:	**Pros:**
Price could increase every year	Price normally guaranteed not to go up
Probably end up at higher cost	Probably end up at lower cost over time
Use it or lose it benefit	Guaranteed benefit to someone
Limited choice of caregivers	Broader choice of caregivers
Usually reimbursement requiring receipts	Usually indemnity and no receipts

As you can see, there is a lot to know about Long-Term Care Insurance, and there is also no one single perfect solution. I highly encourage you to talk to a financial planner about what type of coverage, if any, is the best for your own personal situation. My firm does a weekly radio show about all sorts of financial topics. We turn them into podcasts and have them available on our website. If you want to learn more about comparing types of long-term care coverage, you can find our podcast here* that contains loads of helpful information about this topic.

Don't wait on this–it doesn't get any cheaper and your health usually doesn't get any better! The best age to address Long-term Care insurance is between 55 and 65. You are likely to be in good enough health to obtain a policy if you want to, and the rates at these ages are more favorable.

So how do you translate all of this into strengths and weaknesses in your health care planning? Weaknesses include a lack of knowledge about the prices and your available options. Turn this into a strength by doing the research to determine your options and cost. Another weakness is not knowing if you have enough retirement assets or income to cover the cost

---

* http://www.sterkfinancialservices.com/blog/understanding-long-term-care-insurance

of health insurance or a big health-related expense. Create a strength by filling out your budget tool with the insurance cost information, and setting aside a pool of emergency money to cover any deductible or out-of-pocket expense that could occur. Don't delay retirement because you are afraid you can't afford to bridge the health insurance gap–do your research to find out if you can. Finally, a weakness would be not determining how a long-term illness or care need can impact your spouse. Turn this into a strength by determining how and when to insure against this risk if it is right for you.

Action Steps For Health-Related Planning:

→• Find out if and how long your group coverage can last, and what the price will be.

→• Gather quotes on individual coverage if you need to bridge the gap between group coverage and Medicare.

→• Allot emergency money to cover deductible and out-of-pocket expenses.

→• Understand your Medicare rules and when you need to take action.

→• Determine if you need/want Long-Term Care Insurance and investigate the types and costs to find what is right for you.

CHAPTER 5

IT'S ALL ABOUT THE BENJAMINS!

"I'm starting to worry about my investments. My broker has stopped quoting Warren Buffet and started quoting Jimmy Buffet!"
– Randy Glasbergen

Money, money, money. It's pretty hard to retire without it. While money isn't the only thing that matters during retirement, it's most definitely the mother of all issues. And it certainly creates the most angst, fear, and uncertainty.

Do I have enough to retire? What if I run out of money? Is my portfolio invested the right way? What do I do with my

401k when I retire? What if I love my job? How do I maximize my Social Security? Are my investments actually good ones? Which pension option should I chose?

Meet John and Cindy. John and Cindy hail from sunny California, and both of them wanted to retire early. There was a 12-year age difference between them. John was ready to pull the retirement trigger when he hit 60. Cindy was only 48 at the time, and really enjoyed her job as the director of a non-profit agency supporting domestic violence survivors. She wanted to continue to make an impact on the lives of others through her work. Between the two of them, they had saved around $1.5 million dollars. We spent time visiting about what was most important to them, and how their finances might support an early retirement. We determined together that John and Cindy probably had enough money to retire with confidence because they had set aside enough money to fund the lifestyle they wanted to live. I was able to help them create a strategy to make their retirement assets last. John retired, and Cindy made the decision to work part-time for seven more years, retiring fully at age 55. Cindy was able to use a little known 401(k) loophole to access her retirement plan dollars early without paying the IRA premature withdrawal charge. By leaving her job (separating from service) after she was 55, and withdrawing money directly from the 401k plan itself, she avoided a 10% federal early withdrawal penalty.

John and Cindy are a great example of making a lifestyle choice during retirement vs. a purely monetary choice. They wanted to travel together, and Cindy cutting back to part-time work allowed them time for adventures around the world. Their retirement plan also gave her the ability to continue to make a difference in an area Cindy felt most passionate about. And finally, smart tax strategy let their money work for them, and not for the IRS.

The goal at this stage of retirement planning is to determine the strengths and weaknesses of your retirement money. When you know where your strengths and weakness lie, you can make informed choices about change. You may choose to continue life as it is, or to make an adjustment to part-time work, or to pull the retirement trigger. In any event, knowledge is power, and we have to get a handle on your finances to make a smart choice. The finances are broken down into two separate categories: income and assets.

Income

The income sources you have in retirement create a level of stability. There are many types of income sources, including your Social Security, pensions, annuities, or even part-time work. Your first step in evaluating the strengths and weaknesses in your income is to make a list of what your income sources are, how long they last, and how much continues to your spouse if you die.

At this point, many people shake their heads and say, "Well, how do I know when to take my Social Security?" That is a totally legit question, because as of 2016, there are 567 different combinations of ways a couple can structure their Social Security payouts. No wonder there is confusion!

There is no one right way for everyone. Here are a few rules of thumb to consider:

Social Security Rules Of Thumb

1. You have a normal retirement age. It is based on your year of birth.
2. The government no longer mails everyone a statement. You can find one online at www.ssa.gov.

3. Don't take Social Security early if you plan to earn more than around $16k a year–you will end up paying it back!

4. Each year you wait to take it, up until your age 70, increases your payout by around 8%.

5. You have to live 12-15 years beyond age 70 for the effect of the increased payout to be better than taking the smaller amount at your normal retirement age.

In an environment with 567 choices, it would be difficult to cover all of the nuances of Social Security planning. Rest assured, there IS a way to maximize your payout. Some people nearing retirement chose to visit with a counselor at their local Social Security office. These counselors can often tell you what your options are, but are not trained on actually maximizing your benefit over time. Certain financial planners can forecast the optimal way to take your Social Security benefits by plugging in a few key factors that pertain to you. It is a weakness within your plan to not know your personal best option. Work with someone you trust to turn the uncertainty of Social Security into a strong selection within your retirement plan.

A Word About Pensions

Not everyone is fortunate enough to have a pension. If you are one of the lucky ones, then your Pension Election is very important. Generally speaking, when someone becomes eligible to take their pension, the company will offer them a variety of choices. Sometimes there are quite a few, sometimes just a handful. The three most common options are a Straight Life option, a Joint & Survivor Option, and a Lump Sum option. Unless I was actually creating a retirement plan for you, I don't know which option is right for you. What I do know is that there are some key things to be aware of within each option.

Straight Life - pays out a benefit as long as you live. Once you die, the pension payments are done. If you live until a lovely old age, you have outsmarted the company and gained the highest possible value from your pension. But if you die early, then you and your family lose the very benefits you worked for years to earn.

Joint & Survivor Options - pays out as long as you and one named survivor lives. Usually the only survivor you can name is your spouse. Often times the amount the survivor will get is half of what you had been getting. Typically the amount you receive monthly from this option is quite a bit less than the Straight Life option. Once you both have died, all pension payments cease—no matter how long or short of a time you received them.

Lump Sum - this pays out one single payment, and then you are no longer eligible for monthly pension payments. If you just take the cash, you will owe taxes immediately. If you roll it to an IRA, you can delay taxes until you take money out of the IRA. Not all plans offer a lump sum option. The downside of this option is that if you don't invest wisely, the lump sum may not actually create income for you that lasts a lifetime. The benefit of choosing this option is that you can have a higher level of control over when and how to take income, thus controlling your tax ramifications. You also have control over what happens to the money when you die, as you can set up beneficiary instructions to leave remaining money to anyone that you want to designate.

Having a pension is a retirement strength. Not choosing your payout wisely is a retirement weakness. Taking time to understand what the options mean and how they affect you adds stability and strength to your retirement plan.

The bottom line on income is that the more sources you have, the more stable your retirement outlook becomes. The higher percentage of fixed income sources you have to cover your retirement expenses, the stronger your level of stability is. We call that a "stability ratio." The more you boost your stability ratio with specific income sources, the more likely it is that you will have a successful retirement.

Assets

By the time someone seeks advice from me, they usually have built wealth in a variety of scattered accounts. You may have a significant chunk of your retirement money in a 401(k) through your current employer. You probably also have old 401(k) accounts from previous jobs that you just left there. Perhaps you have a brother-in-law who used to be an advisor, and once upon a time you started a Roth IRA with him. More than likely, you will have a smattering of accounts like a few IRAs, some investment accounts, an E-Trade account from that time you tried your hand at day trading, or that stock you got when your life insurance company went public.

All of your financial decisions probably made good sense at the time. And many of them probably have strong holdings in them now. The problem is that collectively they are not set up to coordinate with each other. This adds risk and creates missed opportunities. These missed opportunities are generally created in three different ways: overlap, poor performance, and skew.

When people have multiple accounts, I frequently see overlap—meaning that the same stock or mutual fund is held in two or three of your accounts. If that holding is a rock star, then you will be quite happy. But if that holding falls on hard times, the effect is multiplied in your portfolio because you hold it in so many places. This overlap creates a level of risk that is simply unnecessary and certainly not strategic.

We also see risk created because people don't really know how to tell if their investments are any good. How do you know if your mutual fund or stock is above average or a dirty dog of a holding? The answer is surprisingly simple. You use a technique called Peer Group Ranking.

Listen, no one can control the ups and downs of the market. No one can time things perfectly to buy and sell at the exact right time to always avoid loss and always capture gain. So what can you control? You can control monitoring how your investment is doing against every other investment with similar risk and type. That is what Peer Group Ranking is all about.

Here is how it works. You start by buying a service, like Morningstar, for example, that quantifies and ranks data. Morningstar breaks mutual funds down into categories by size and similar investment strategy. For instance, there are over 2700 available mutual funds in the world that are considered large company growth funds–all investing in stocks of a certain size and style. Next, Morningstar ranks the performance of all of the funds in the same category against each other. 1% would be best performers and 100% would be the worst performers. It stands to reason, then, that the 50th percentile is exactly average. Morningstar ranks them for a recent period, like year to date. It also ranks them historically, like the last one-, three-, five-, and 10-year periods.

You can use Morningstar Peer Group Ranking to determine if your fund's performance is consistently above average or not. Look up your fund, and look at the Peer Group Percentages. If your fund is consistently falling between 1% and 40%, then your fund is consistently above average. Fabulous! If your fund is consistently ranking between 40% and 60%, then your fund is average. Not fabulous, but not horrible either. However, if your fund is consistently falling to rankings between 60% and 100%, then you know your results are well below average. If that is the case, you need to ask yourself why you would continue to hold a below-average performer when there are 2,700 options available to choose from.

Now I am not suggesting that Peer Group Ranking is the one and only way to evaluate the strength of your portfolio, but it is a dynamic tool that can be used to determine the good, the bad, and the ugly of what lives in your portfolio. The bottom line is that consistent poor performance obviously impacts your returns. The point of good investing is to get the highest return for whatever level of risk you are willing to take. Poor performance translates to less income and assets available in retirement, thus the missed opportunities that I am talking about.

The final missed opportunity that I want to cover has to do with balance within your portfolio. More often than not, portfolios have areas in which they are more heavily invested than is ideal. It stands to reason that if you are overweighted in certain areas, then you must be underweighted in other areas. If those underweighted (or even non-existent!) areas in the market are the strongest performers, then you have missed an opportunity for capturing growth.

This imbalance of being overweighted, underweighted, or missing asset classes is called "skew." Ultimately it damages long-term portfolio returns. Simply put, you make less money. How do you fix this? Remember that personal Risk Tolerance Quiz you took in chapter 2? You fix your portfolio imbalances by creating a strategy that aligns your asset allocation with your personal Risk Tolerance level.

What the heck is asset allocation? It's just the way you break your money down into different sizes and styles, called asset classes. Asset allocation is also known as diversification. There is a science to asset allocation that was based on Modern Portfolio Theory (MPT). In a nutshell, MPT suggests that for any level of risk that you are willing to take, there is a best possible return percentage. This best possible outcome is scientifically calculated by blending the amounts you invest inside of these different asset classes in certain ways.

Many financial advisors and investment firms take this one step further. They start with MPT, and then overlay current economic conditions to make tweaks to the blend. If you are a do-it-your-selfer with your portfolio, you can Google "asset allocation for your personal Risk Tolerance Level" and find many guides to help you determine how to break down your money. If you have no interest in figuring this out on your own, then hire a financial advisor you trust to help you make your asset allocation decisions.

To recap, the strength of your portfolio assets comes from a correctly diversified asset allocation, and by using holdings that have long-term, above average results. Portfolio weakness comes from overlap, investing in poor performers, and having skew in certain areas. You can reduce your risk and eliminate missed opportunities by aligning your asset allocation with your personal risk tolerance level. Take time to analyze your allocation and holdings in order to develop a strategy for your retirement assets with a higher level of strength.

The financial piece of your retirement puzzle comes down to income and assets. You can begin to answer many of your own questions by mapping out where income will come from and how high your stability ratio is. By avoiding overlap, poor performers, and skew, you can take your portfolio to a stronger level. The strength of this financial position will help you make informed decisions about your readiness to pull the retirement trigger.

Action Steps For Evaluating Your Income and Assets:

→• Make a list of your retirement income sources, how long they last, and how much continues to your spouse if you die.

→• Investigate and choose your best Social Security and pension payout option.

→• Look through your portfolio holdings to determine where there is overlap and skew.

→• Analyze the performance of each holding and note what is strong and what is weak.

→• Determine your ideal asset allocation strategy.

CHAPTER 6
TIME TO STRATEGIZE!

"You want me to get my ducks in a row? I'd settle for them being in the same pond!"
- Anonymous

Oh, my gosh, we have made it to my favorite part—it's strategy time! First, you created your money philosophy and really thought about what retirement will look and feel like. Next, you created a cash flowchart for yourself using the budget tool. After that you took a long hard look at your current situation from several perspectives—health, legacy, risk, and money. This is my favorite part because we get to use the work you have done to create possibilities for your future. This is your reward for taking time to slog through all of the nitty gritty details. Creating strategy is an art. It's time to pull all of that work and all of those details into a plan that will show you the exact moment that work becomes optional. Your strategy will show you how and when you can retire with confidence!

Let me make a quick disclaimer here: there a dozens of ways to set up a strong retirement plan. There are many different strategies that might make sense. I can't give you specific advice in a general setting like this book. But what I can do is help you connect all of the work you have done so far with one option that could be a meaningful strategy for you. I want you to see a pathway that can propel you toward a confident retirement. Of course, one size does not fit all. If you want a more personalized plan, then reach out to a financial planner for professional help. If you feel comfortable doing it yourself, than I want to give you the tools to understand the components and the scope of a strong strategy.

Money Strategy

It's time to tie a few things together. Remember that budget tool from chapter 2? Now it's time to take your notes about the income sources you uncovered from chapter 5 and add that to your budget tool. You previously listed all of your expenses.

Now we will add your fixed income sources. When you do this, you will immediately see if your fixed income sources cover your expenses. If they do, that's a fantastic start! If they don't, then you have an Income Gap.

An Income Gap is very common for most people entering retirement. Having an Income Gap does not mean you need to delay retirement, it simply means that you have to create a strategy in which pieces of your portfolio are used to plug the gap.

I shared with you in chapter 2 the differences between fixed expenses and variable expenses, and why that is important. The budget tool should clearly note which expenses are fixed–meaning they don't really change much month to month, or year to year. You also should be able to easily see which expenses are variable–meaning they are likely to shift and change as you age.

Here is where the data from your budget tool turns into strategy. This is where we answer the question, "How do I make sure I never run out of money?" There is actually a very simple solution to this complex problem. I call this solution the Fixed-With-Fixed strategy.

The Fixed-With-Fixed strategy aligns your fixed expenses with your fixed income sources. Ideally, you want the income sources that are designed to last your lifetime to be large enough to cover your fixed expenses. If the sources last a lifetime, than you can confidently know your basic needs are covered for a lifetime. See how that works?

What if there is a Fixed Income Gap? Then it may make sense to take a portion of your retirement portfolio and invest it in a way that creates additional fixed income. This can be done through a variety of investment vehicles such as CDs, certain types of bonds, annuities, etc. If you know your Fixed Income Gap, you can use that monthly number to dial in the exact minimum amount of your portfolio necessary to invest in these vehicles to provide you the desired gap-filling income.

For example, Jerry and Linda went through this very process. Jerry had served his Midwestern community as a family physician for decades, and Linda had helped part-time managing the office. They wanted to create a strategy for retirement that would leave them feeling secure and comfortable. After plugging in their projected expenses and income sources into the budget tool, they found a Fixed Income Gap of $1,000 per month. We visited with Jerry and Linda about a variety of tools they could use to provide themselves with the necessary money each month to plug the gap. Jerry took $300,000 of his retirement assets and invested it into a program that provided a fixed lifetime income of $1,000 a month. Now they had a Fixed-With-

Fixed strategy in place and felt confident that they would never run out of money.

But what about inflation? There are two ways to address this. First, some fixed income investment vehicles do have the potential to increase in order to offset inflation. Currently, Social Security programs occasionally get an increase based on the cost of living. Unfortunately, most corporate pensions do not offer increases, but certain government- or state-related ones sometimes do. If you choose to invest in other Fixed Income investment vehicles, you need to find out if they offer inflation-adjusted payouts. If they don't, then you have to plan to pull money later from the rest of your liquid portfolio to fill the gap created by inflation.

Once you have plugged your Fixed Income Gap with additional fixed income sources, it is time to turn your attention to the rest of your portfolio. One downside of a Fixed-With-Fixed strategy is that money allocated to plug the gaps is usually not easily accessible if you have an unexpected need arise. Fixed programs tend to trade off access to large chunks of the money in exchange for lifetime income. Therefore, the rest of your portfolio should have a very strong focus on liquidity.

Liquidity Strategy

Liquidity means access to your money. You need to have a pool of money that you can get to any time, any day, for any reason, without any penalty. This liquid pool of money is designed to do a few things for you:

1. Cover any emergencies that come up
2. Cover your variable expenses
3. Cover your occasional expenses
4. Plug the Inflation Gap later in retirement

The whole key to liquid investing is that it allows for flexibility. Your life will shift and change throughout retirement. You need a significant portion of your portfolio to be able to shift and change with you. There are a variety of investment vehicles such as bank accounts, mutual funds, stocks, bonds, and managed accounts that are considered liquid, but it's well beyond the scope of this book to discuss the intricacies of them all (otherwise this would be as large as those crazy prospectuses you hate getting in the mail!). Needless to say, do your homework. If there is a penalty that you have to pay to the investment company when you take your money out, then that investment vehicle is NOT liquid.

Retirement assets that have not been spoken for in your Fixed-With-Fixed strategy should be allocated to your liquid pool. Once you know which assets these are, then you want to apply the lessons you learned in chapter 5 about overlap, performance, and skew.

Before you pull the retirement trigger, you need to reallocate your liquid assets into the asset allocation model that matches with your personal Risk Tolerance level. Begin by clearing out the holdings that are weak performers. Once you have sold or removed the holdings that have poor performance history, you can take the remaining holdings and plug them into your asset allocation model. If you find that you are low in certain asset classes, then you know where to add holdings to round out your asset allocation strategy. If you find that you are heavy in certain asset classes, then lower your amount of holdings in that asset class—even if they are strong performers. It's kind of like putting together a jigsaw puzzle; each holding belongs in a certain spot. Making these changes will help eliminate the overlap and skew that can add unnecessary risk and create missed opportunities.

As you make changes to your portfolio, be mindful that selling different holdings may create a taxable event for you. Check with your CPA if you are not sure how that will affect you, so you don't get hit with an unexpected nasty tax surprise!

Once you have determined your Income Gap, built your Fixed-With-Fixed Strategy, and reallocated your liquid portfolio, you can move on to the next part of your overall retirement strategy.

Risk Strategy

It's time to take action on the things you researched surrounding risk and insurance in chapter 3. It is important to meet with your insurance agent at this stage and make sure your auto, home, and umbrella coverages are set up with the right limits to protect you.

It is also important to know where the Income Gaps are for your spouse if you should pass away. Consider adding life insurance coverage to offset the loss of a Social Security or pension check if you die. Consider removing coverage if your Fixed Income Sources are more than adequate to take care of a surviving spouse.

This is also your opportunity to make a determination about long-term care. If you have decided to layer Long-Term Care Insurance into your retirement plan, you are likely considering the hybrid option that doubles as a life insurance policy. This hybrid death benefit should be factored into the total amount of life insurance that you carry. If you have a life insurance policy that is not a hybrid and does not provide the dual long-term care benefit, then evaluate the potential of adding a hybrid policy and dropping your existing coverage. I am not suggesting everyone go out willy-nilly and replace all of their good life insurance policies. I am suggesting you evaluate your total need, analyze what you currently have, and make an educated decision about what type and kind of insurance to carry during your retirement.

Health Strategy

If you have done the research suggested in chapter 4, then deploying this part of your strategy should be simple. When you retire, either:

1. Extend your group coverage
2. Take out individual coverage
3. Get yourself set up on Medicare

If you decided not to pursue Long-Term Care insurance, then confidently put that issue to bed. If you made a choice to add that to your retirement strategy, then take the steps to put a policy into place. Both Traditional and Hybrid polices require underwriting. I suggest that you choose the policy type that best suits your situation, and begin the underwriting before your pull the retirement trigger. Why before?

Amy was 62 and lives in the Carolinas. Her husband, who had always handled the finances, passed away six years earlier. Amy had spent a lot of time working with us. It was very important to her that she understand how investment vehicles worked, what the fees were, and why she should use different options. It was all new to her when she started, but now, after educating herself, she felt like she had a really strong grasp on things. Together, they had saved around $750,000 in retirement dollars. Her husband also left a small amount of money in life insurance proceeds when he passed away. Amy liked her job as an executive assistant, but now at 62 was ready to consider retirement.

Amy had plenty of money to cover her retirement needs for the lifestyle she wanted to live, and also felt she had enough money to cover a long-term care stay if needed. But Amy had a very strong sense of wanting to protect her assets for her children. She was not willing to let an extended care stay eat through the portfolio she and her husband had worked years to build. As part of her retirement strategy,

Amy decided to take out a long-term care policy in order to protect her assets for her children.

When we went through the underwriting process, I got a call from the company that the policy would be postponed. They had found an issue in her underwriting tests that required surgical follow-up from her doctors. I relayed this to Amy, and she began a six-month journey of handling the medical issue that prior to underwriting she had known nothing about. Amy decided to delay retirement during this six-month period because it was unknown how this unexpected health issue would impact her life and finances in the future. Fortunately, the surgery removed the health threat, Amy got her Long-Term Care in place, and then confidently pulled the retirement trigger.

Stories like this illustrate why it is ideal to get any insurance into place prior to pulling the retirement trigger. Is it mandatory? Of course not. It's simply a good idea. If something unexpected comes up, then you have time to decide if and how that impacts your long-term retirement strategy. I think that having all of your insurance ducks in a row before you pull the retirement trigger adds strength to your overall plan.

Estate Strategy

Talking about getting documents done is one thing. Getting them done is another. People often ask me if they can create the documents themselves. The short answer to that is yes. The smart answer to that is no.

It is absolutely possible to download templates of wills, powers of attorney, and trusts from the internet. If you sign them in front of a notary, they generally are valid. It is certainly a less expensive route to go. But my opinion is that you get what you pay for.

The law is complex. Each state has different nuances, guidelines, and language that pertain to estate planning. If you want a good estate plan, I suggest you hire a good attorney to create your documents.

That being said, there are ways to keep the cost of estate-planning documents down. If you go prepared, and know what you want the documents to accomplish, you cut down on the time the attorney spends in discussion with you. Take time ahead to decide who to name as executor, or who should be the guardian of your minor children, or how you want the family farm to pass down. Listen to their advice on whether a trust makes sense for you. Don't use your attorney as a counselor to flush out your estate dreams and wishes. Do use them as a conduit to take the dreams and wishes you have already decided upon, and make them legally binding.

So book the appointment, arrive prepared, and at the very minimum get your three-pack of documents created or revised. Have your Will, Financial Power of Attorney, and Health Care Power of Attorney in place before you pull the retirement trigger.

Overall, your retirement strategy should pull quite a number of things together. Your Money Philosophy has informed your personal risk tolerance level. Your budget tool laid out the framework to map out a plan for fixed and liquid assets. Your reallocation aligned your retirement assets with your risk level, decreasing risk and avoiding missed opportunities. Your money, risk, health, and estate-planning pieces have been put into place in a meaningful and thoughtful manner. You now know if you have reached the point where work has become optional.

The strategy you just created addresses the big three areas of focus that contribute to a successful retirement: emotional readiness, health-related issues, and financial factors. As I said earlier, a high level of retirement confidence comes from having your ducks in a row in all three of these areas. By creating this strategy to maximize them all, you have gotten one giant step closer to that retirement mecca!

Action Steps For Creating Your Strategy:
(Part 1)

→• Add your retirement income sources to the Budget Tool to determine any Income Gap.

→• Cover fixed expenses with fixed income. If there is a gap, investigate ways to re-position a part of your portfolio to create more fixed income.

→• Keep the rest of your portfolio liquid to address variable spending patterns, occasional expenses, and future infla-tion gaps.

→• Reallocate your portfolio to fix overlap, skew, and performance weakness; and to align with your personal risk tolerance level.

Action Steps For Creating Your Strategy:
(Part 2)

→• Align your liability insurances with the correct limits.

→• Add or remove life insurance to take care of your spouse's retirement income needs and/or your legacy goals.

→• Determine if Long-Term Care Insurance is right for you and put a policy in place.

→• Deploy a health insurance solution based on your research.

CHAPTER 7

SHAKY TRIGGER FINGER?

"Behind every retired man is a wife wishing he would go back to work!"

- Anonymous

Congratulations on making it this far in your retirement planning journey! You have done a lot of research. You have clarity on your strengths and weaknesses. You know if work has become optional. You have a framework built for retirement strategy. Yet chances are, there is still a churning in your gut. A little nagging voice saying "Am I really ready? Am I sure?"

I get it! Even the best-laid plans can veer off track, and the very possibility of that can create a load of anxiety. My goal is for you to be able to pull the retirement trigger with confidence. So let's explore some things that might be getting in the way of you doing just that.

I have worked with hundreds and hundreds of clients over the years. In my experience, there are four main things that get in the way of people pulling the retirement trigger–even if they have a well thought-out and solid plan. These four things all attack your confidence. They shed doubt on your retirement decision. So let's get them out in the open and explore some ways to turn these momentum killers into your opportunity to make a positive and exciting change. The four reasons are: The Overwhelm Trap, The Stuck Spouse, The Fear Of Getting Ripped Off Phenomenon, and The Pit Of What If.

The Overwhelm Trap

- ☐ Oh, my gosh, there is so much to know! How can I possibly learn all of this?
- ☐ I get the basics, but what if I have no interest in learning all of the details? Do I have to?

☐ I really just want to live my life and ignore this because it's too much to handle. But is that smart?

If you find yourself asking these type of questions, then you are stuck in the Overwhelm Trap. No doubt about it: if done correctly, retirement planning has complexity. The worst part of overwhelm is that it typically leads to paralysis. It creates an environment where it's easier to stick your head in the sand and ignore the issue instead of taking action. You have three solutions to escape from this trap.

1. Immersion Education. It is totally possible for you to learn all things money. Take a class online, enroll in finance courses at your local university, or self-educate through books. The data is out there and available for anyone to learn.

2. Bite-Size Learning. If you would rather pull your eyelashes out than immerse yourself in financial education, consider a Bite-Size Learning approach. Read a book like this, go to a local retirement seminar, or listen to an online webinar about retirement planning and investing. Get familiar with the highlights of the most important topics.

3. Hire Help. Unless you are a dedicated Do-It-Yourselfer, you may want to consider hiring help. Even if you are, you may want to have someone give your plan a second opinion–just to be on the safe side. Certified Financial Planners™ like me spend their career immersed in education, building experience, analyzing investments, sharing wisdom, and creating strategy. If you would feel more confident with a collaborative partner, than consider hiring an expert to help.

The Stuck Spouse Problem

☐ I want to retire and spend more time with my husband, but I don't know how to talk to him about this stuff. I barely understand it myself. How do I begin that conversation?

☐ My wife is terrified that if we stop working, we might run out of money–even though we have saved a lot. How do I convince her that we will be ok?

☐ I'm getting tired, but my husband loves his job. How do we transition together and keep both of us happy?

☐ I get the basics, but my wife has never handled the money and really doesn't want to. Neither one of us are experts, so we just keep working. How do we change that?

If you are married, it will come as no surprise to learn that most couples are not on the exact same page when it comes to money. Usually one is a saver and one is a spender. Often one spouse handles the money and the other one is very happy not to. Frequently one spouse is ready to consider retirement, and the other spouse does not even want to discuss it. How do you bridge these gaps?

It all comes down to effective communication. The good news is that there are a few techniques unique to retirement planning that can be helpful. If you want to retire and your spouse is stuck–be it stuck in ignorance, confusion, or downright stubbornness–try these ideas.

1. Feed The Right Questions. Telling someone what to do is often met with resistance. Asking someone's opinion, instead, can create more openness. Use the sections in this book to ask your spouse specific questions. Instead of telling your husband, "Honey, we should retire" try asking, "How do you see us spending time together when we retire?" or, "I know you used to love

woodworking. Do you see yourself spending more time with that once we retire?" By asking questions, you've opened the door to a conversation about your–and your spouse's–Money Philosophy.

2. Collaborate Through Conversation. Instead of telling your wife in a patronizing tone, "Don't worry, we should be fine," ask her, "How often will you want to travel to see our grandkids when we retire?" or "Do you see us living in the same house when we retire, or are you thinking about something different?" By asking these questions, you are zeroing in on your Fixed and Variable Income needs. Each section in this book can be a guide for you to have great conversations about retirement, money, and what you both value in life.

3. Give Them This Book–with sticky "love" notes in it. Don't ask them to read the whole thing. Just ask them to look at the parts that mean the most to you. Make your love note more meaningful by writing about why you want them to read that page or that chapter. I strongly recommend that one of your sticky notes be in the Money Philosophy section–because that is where your plan's meaning and value really begins. Maybe that note will say, "I want to travel the world with you while we are still young enough to have adventures!" Perhaps

your note next to the Fixed-With-Fixed Strategy will say, "Honey, I never want you to worry about running out of money. Here is a way to fix that." Or maybe your "love" note in the Long-Term Care area will say, "Blech! If I ever lose my marbles, I want you and the kids to put me up in style!" Make it lighthearted. Make it sound like you. Make sure it comes across with love.

4. Book The Appointment. Sometimes you just have to get it done. Gather your data, interview planners, and book an appointment to enlist professional help. Start the process, and go through the details of your finances with a planner on your own. Loop your spouse in on the most critical parts of a plan—the lifestyle and the actual strategy. This plan allows for forward movement toward retirement without requiring too much time and effort from a stuck spouse.

The Fear Of Getting Ripped Off Phenomenon

☐ I want to hire help, but how do I know if someone's advice is best for them, or best for me?

☐ All my financial advisor wants to do is talk about some product they can sell me. How do I actually get unbiased strategies and advice?

☐ I wonder how much commission they are making off of me?

☐ Our advisor is my husband's golfing buddy, but I always feel like he talks down to me. What can I do instead?

☐ I'm pretty sure I have gotten ripped off before and made a bad investment decision once upon a time. How do I make sure that doesn't happen again?

☐ I hate attorneys and I don't trust financial advisors. They all just want my money. Where do I turn for help?

Let's face it. The financial industry has gotten enough black eyes that anyone in their right mind would be suspicious. Misleading sales practices, corporate shenanigans, and blatant fraud have dominated the headlines. It's no wonder that you don't know who to trust.

If you want to hire help but are afraid of getting ripped off, here are a few important things to consider:

How Does Your Financial Planner Make Their Money?

An advisor makes money one of two ways: either through fees or commissions. Bottom line, financial advising is not a non-profit business. Your advisor brings wisdom and experience to the table, and expects to be compensated for the help they provide you. Is one of these ways better? I think so, and here is why.

When I started in this industry 20+ years ago, the normal way to work with people was to sell a product and earn a commission. But people were not looking for financial products to buy, they were looking for advice and strategies about what to do. The problem was that most financial advisors only made money one way–when they sold you a financial product. So inherently there was, and in many cases still is, a competing agenda within the relationship. You want advice and strategies, and the advisor is just trying to sell you something so they can make a commission.

I wanted to create an environment where we always had the same agenda as the client. I want our clients to always feel that we have their best interests at heart, and to never worry that the only reason we're recommending a course of action is so that we can sell them something. The only way I can do that is to simply charge a fee for my time, wisdom, and advice. Therefore, many years ago, we evolved into a planning practice that is primarily fee-based instead of commission-based.

So how do fees typically work in a fee-based setting? Fees take into account two things: time and complexity. Based on an initial conversation, your planner will determine the amount of time it will take to create a strategic plan for you. The more complex your situation, the higher your fee will be. A typical retirement plan fee generally ranges between one to five thousand dollars.

Normally, the planning fee is broken into two parts. I have found that most financial planners charge half of the fee up front, at the time they have you sign a financial planning contract that outlines the scope of the work you're hiring them to do. The remaining half of the fee may be charged when the plan is complete, or, in certain situations, may actually be waived.

The beauty of working with a fee-based planner is that you can take their recommendations and advice, and go back to your existing advisors to implement it. When the plan is done, they collect the back half of your fee. The strategies that they suggest are unbiased, objective, and based on the best course of action for you—no matter how or where you implement them. You are paying them to create a retirement strategy, and it is never based on them selling you a financial product. Can you see how that creates an experience where you can trust their advice?

Sometimes through the planning process, people feel an enhanced level of trust and collaboration with their fee-based planner. They determine that they DO want to have their fee-based planner manage assets or help them with insurance. If that's the case, your planner should explain exactly how they will be compensated. In most cases, when a fee-based planner helps you implement your investment or insurance strategy, the revenue generated from implementing your plan is used to offset and waive the back half of the fee. You see, I don't think it's fair to double dip–your planner shouldn't get paid to create a strategy, and then paid again to implement the same strategy!

The bottom line is this: with a fee-based arrangement, you will walk away with a plan and a strategy that is good advice no matter what. You will know that the recommendations are solid regardless of whether you do any further business with them or not. If you choose to–great! If not–also great! But either way, you get what you came for: advice and strategies about what to do going forward so you feel confident taking steps toward your financial future.

Let me also make note of something here. When/if you chose to do further business with a financial planner, it is their job to place your investments or insurance programs into the financial vehicles that are right for you. Sometimes, vehicles are fee-based and require your advisor to have a special license to utilize them. Sometimes, vehicles are commission-based and don't have the option to pay your advisor in a fee-based way. Not all financial vehicles are available to planners who are only fee-based, or who are only commission-based. But they are all available to a planner who has a hybrid model.

A hybrid model means that if you are engaging a planner to actually manage your investment or insurance, they can make recommendations from either side–fee-based or commission-based. A hybrid advisor has access to a broader array of financial vehicles and therefore can make a more targeted recommendation about what is right for you. To avoid any type of "bait-and-switch" issue of an advisor moving from a fee-based approach to a commission-based approach without your awareness, just be sure that they disclose how they are compensated for each and every vehicle that they recommend.

Is Your Planner Working For You Or For The Insurance Company?

Here's the skinny on this. If an insurance company's name is on the door of the office, then your planner probably is an agent for that company. What does that mean to you?

There is a vast difference between an independent financial advisor and an agent representing a company. An independent advisor assesses your situation, and matches you up with the best solutions in the financial industry. The role of an agent in a company is to match you up with the best solution that particular insurance company offers. Big difference. Be aware, and be wary.

Do They Make You Feel Stupid?

Finance can be frighteningly complex. But it doesn't have to be. Finding a good planner who can explain difficult concepts in a way that you easily understand is like finding a hidden gem. How do you find them? Interview them.

The format of an interview should go like this:

- ☐ Bring nothing. An interview is a conversation over coffee, not a time to go over statements or planning.
- ☐ You tell them why you are interviewing planners and a little about yourself.
- ☐ They tell you their process for working with people and what the fee would be.
- ☐ You evaluate whether you feel a positive connection or feel talked down to, and determine if this person would bring you value.
- ☐ Thank them for their time and let them know you will get back to them if you want to proceed.

I suggest you interview at least four planners. At least one of them should have a local presence, and at least one of them should have a national presence. For some people, sitting across the table from a local advisor makes them feel the most comfortable. Why a national firm? The beauty of the world today is that we are all interconnected by this marvelous tool called the internet. Online relationships are formed every day–why not one with just the right financial planner? (Not gonna lie–I hope you interview mine! We are really darn good at this!) A national planner will have the appropriate licenses in all of the states, and a technologically friendly way to conduct meetings with clients no matter where they live.

Interviewing a financial planner can feel a little daunting to some people. You may not know exactly what questions to ask. In our Strategic Retirement Tool Kit*, we have included a list of questions as a guide to conduct your interviews. This Financial Planner Evaluation Tool can help you feel confident you're connecting with a planner who has your best interests at heart, is collaborative, and has a process that will meet your specific needs.

Meet with your local advisor at their office. Evaluate how the environment physically feels to you. Is it classy or shabby? Are

---

* http://www.sterkfinancialservices.com/p/toolkit

the magazines up to date or old? Does it feel warm and inviting, or cold and sterile? Is their planning process written down so you can understand and follow along? Do you understand how they make money and what the fees are? Do you feel this would be a collaborative relationship? Go through your interview. See how you feel.

Meet with a planner from a national advisory firm online. Most national firms will have a web-type set-up and they can show you how to link up. Typically, you can see them, and also see any materials they have to show you. You can do all of this from the comfort of your own home. Evaluate the background of the planner's office that you can see online. Does it look well-kept, or are there piles of paper all over the desk? Did it feel like you were actually having a conversation with them or were they distracted? Do you understand how they work with people and their fees? Are you clear on how to send and receive information from them during the planning process? Do you feel that the level of collaboration and expertise outweighs the benefits of a local office? Go through your interview. See how you feel.

Make a decision.

The Pit Of What If?

The biggest single reason people procrastinate over pulling the retirement trigger is because they are mired in The Pit Of What If.

- ☐ What if something unexpected happens?
- ☐ What if my plan wasn't truly solid?
- ☐ What if I want to do something different, like retire earlier?
- ☐ What if I die?
- ☐ What if I get divorced?

The What Ifs can go on and on and on....

Bottom line–you cannot outguess the What Ifs. By their very nature, they are unexpected, unforeseen, and unknown. So how can you feel confident about retiring in the face of What Ifs? You forecast a few of them and create a range of possibility, which usually includes a potential best and worst case scenario. Then you decide if you can live with that worst case.

A strong financial plan will take these What Ifs into consideration. In fact, this is one of my own personal favorite parts of planning. Why? Because this is where I see the largest boost of confidence for my clients.

If you choose to hire a fee-based planner, they will show you the long-term impact of various choices. For example: if you do nothing, this is what it looks like; if you make these changes, here is how it improves; if something unexpected happens, like a death or a divorce, here is how it plays out in your future; if you want to retire earlier, later, or work part-time, then this is what you can anticipate.

They say knowledge is power. The uncertainty surrounding the impact of a What If is that causes us to stay stuck in a pit of anxiety and inaction. When you can see, in a strategic forecast, the impact a What If has on your life, it takes the murky fear right out of it. If you just can't live with that worst case scenario, then you have not found the point yet where work has become optional. But if you CAN live with it, then you can break free from the Pit Of What If and confidently pull the retirement trigger.

Action Steps For Your Shaky Trigger Finger:

- → Eliminate feeling overwhelmed by educating yourself or hiring help.

- → Unstick your spouse through strong communication.

- → If you hire help, find an advisor who is fee-based, independent, and collaborative.

- → Forecast your What Ifs to boost your retirement confidence.

CHAPTER 8

CONFIDENTLY PULL THE RETIREMENT TRIGGER

"It's true money can't buy happiness, but I'd cheer up much faster while sitting poolside in a lounge chair outside of my oceanfront mansion!"

– Anonymous

Craig and JoAnne are part of a farm family from Nebraska. Craig grew up on the same land that he raised his own children on. JoAnne worked in town as a teacher's aide. They had both reached 65, and were thinking about what came next in life. Some years, times had been tough. Grain prices, weather, and taxes often took their toll. For much of their life, extra money went toward the kids' sports, braces, giving to their church, and college costs. But Craig and JoAnne had always done two things—funded their IRAs and paid down their debt. The farm was paid off, Social Security was turned on, and cash flow was suddenly not so tight.

As we created a plan, it became evident that between Social Security, JoAnne's school pension, IRAs, and the farm income, all of their needs and more could be taken care of. I created several planning scenarios for Craig showing him that if he rented out the land, they would easily be able to cover all of their fixed and variable expenses. I also developed a potential strategy to use extra income to benefit their church and secure a nice tax deduction. No doubt about it—work had become optional, and they could retire with confidence.

Craig and JoAnne spent a lot of time talking about what mattered most to them. At the end of the planning, they smiled at each other and made a decision that left them both happy. JoAnne would retire, and start taking her pension. She would happily spend time with their children and grandchildren, and helping out around the farm. But Craig was going to keep actively farming—not because he had to, but because he loved to. Craig's heart was on the farm. Their legacy was their land. And he wanted to spend as many years as he could nurturing the crops, tending the farm, and creating a lasting impact on his family farm for generations to come.

In another area of the country, Jeff and Cindy were sitting on their balcony looking out at the crystal blue of the Florida gulf waters. They had recently purchased their new condo in anticipation of wintering someplace warm. Jeff had a big corporate job for a firm in Ohio, where they lived. Cindy was a stay-at-home mom for most of their marriage, raising their three beautiful kids. Jeff's income had increased significantly over the years, and although they lived a very nice lifestyle, they didn't consider themselves extravagant. He had been maxing out his 401(k) for years, and between retirement accounts and a joint investment account they had accumulated over $5 million.

When Jeff was 60 and Cindy was 58, cancer struck. Cindy began a battle with breast cancer that was difficult and scary. After a year full of surgeries, chemo, and radiation, Cindy was pronounced in remission. Jeff reached out to me and said, "I've always loved my job, but my wife matters more. I want to spend whatever time we have left on this earth spending time together. How do we make that happen?"

They gathered their data, and we put together a plan. I created a retirement strategy that showed with a few lifestyle changes, work had become optional, and without hesitation they pulled the retirement trigger. Jeff and Cindy now spend summers toodling around the country in their RV, and winters enjoying the warm sun at their Florida condo.

These are two different real-life scenarios that illustrate an important point: once work becomes optional, retirement is a choice. There are valid reasons for choosing to retire, and reasons that are just as valid to keep working. A well thought-out plan can help you understand if a comfortable retirement is possible, but it's ultimately up to you to decide what the best choice is for your own life.

***

Reading a book can give you knowledge, but the information is useless without action. When you close this book, I want you to make some decisions.

Will you stick your head back in the sand, or will you take action? You can do whatever your heart desires. If that means putting this book on the shelf and consciously choosing not to create a plan, then so be it. This advice will still be relevant whenever you are ready to take a step. Just remember: ignoring or hiding from retirement confusion is like taking a cross country road trip with no map. You might someday end up at the destination you were originally heading for, but the journey there will be fraught with detours, roadblocks, and wrong turns!

Will you use the education you have gained from this book to do it all yourself, or will you hire someone to help you through the process? If you do it all yourself, schedule time to actually address each necessary item. Make sure you have the stamina to get through all of the planning, the expertise to analyze options, and the experience to translate your research into a strategy. If you hire help, schedule your Financial Planner interviews—at least one local, independent, fee-based advisor, and at least one national, independent, fee-based firm.

Is work optional for me right now? A good plan will show you the the timeframe when work becomes optional. Your emotional readiness, health-related issues, and financial components all line up to create your retirement mecca. Are you there yet?

Once work has become optional, will I choose to work longer because I simply want to, or will I choose to pull the retirement trigger? Ahhh, the million dollar question. The answer ties right back to your Money Philosophy. You have mapped out what matters to you. You have carefully considered what you want to spend time doing. Do you want to use the money you have to gain years of doing exactly what you want? Remember, the only thing that money really does is buy you choices. If you choose to work, do it because you truly want to. If you choose to retire, do so with confidence.

It's decision time! Are you ready to retire with a sense of confidence and excitement? A strong retirement plan can lay the groundwork for a successful retirement lifestyle, but only you can make the final decision. Only you can know if you are truly ready.

My hope for you is that by reading this book, you'll begin to see the path toward the retirement you dream of. I want you to understand the important steps you must take as you approach the next phase of life. You have flushed out your personal Money Philosophy. We have addressed the fears that lurk in the back of your mind. I have armed you with the necessary tools to aid in determining current strengths and weaknesses. We have explored the challenges that foster paralysis, and created solutions that bring action. You know if work has become optional. I have given you a strategic framework to build a retirement plan that works. The tools you need are all in your hands.

Are you ready to confidently pull the exciting, life-changing, oh-so-momentous retirement trigger?

Action Step:

→• Pull the trigger!

ACKNOWLEDGEMENTS

firmly believe that no one gets to where they are all on their own. In my own journey, I've been fortunate to encounter a number of people along the way who have inspired me, enlightened me, and made an impact.

I thank my Sterk Financial Services Team. Your unique blend of expertise and exceptional attitude has created an environment that is unique in today's world. Your tireless efforts to care for clients and each other is what makes our company truly thrive.

I express gratitude to mentors and teachers I have had the opportunity to learn from: Scott Carlson, Dan Sullivan, Tonya Leigh Rising, and Brooke Castillo. You all have made an impact in my understanding of what is possible in this life, and given me the courage to go after it.

I send thanks to my parents, Frank and Jane Ellen Colella, who taught me the value of work, family, and doing what is right. To my mom, who watched my kids while I worked and got back on my feet. To my dad, for the lessons on the fundamentals of economics!

I thank my lucky stars daily for the connection and support of the love of my life, Darlo Jansen. Your unwavering kindness and philosophy of giving has helped me be a better person.

I am so grateful for my three children and one grandson–Mace, Marena, Calvin, and Trace. The meaning of life is wrapped up in one word: family. I am so thankful that you are all a part of mine.

ABOUT THE AUTHOR

Author's photo courtesy of KJ Photography

Mary Sterk, CFP®, is the owner of Sterk Financial Services in Dakota Dunes, SD. Mary's inspirational story of fighting her way from Welfare to Wealth Management has motivated many people to believe that anything is possible. She built a better future despite a teenage pregnancy, living in low-income housing, and raising two small children without child support and while subsisting on food stamps. Her quote, "If I can achieve this, anyone can!", has inspired women throughout the country to strive for their own bright future.

Sterk Financial Services (www.sterkfinancialservices.com) specializes in providing strategic direction and personal meaning for client's financial decisions through their unique planning programs. Their radio show, *Money Guide With Mary Sterk,* educates and inspires listeners to create their best financial future.

Mary has been in the investment and insurance industry since 1994, and earned her Certified Financial Planner ™ certification through the American College in Bryn Mawr, PA. Mary also has an artistic side, and has created uplifting messages of hope through her art via Just Mary Designs (www. justmarydesigns.com). In her down time, Mary enjoys spending time with her three children and one grandson, and flying her Piper Cherokee.

In 2006 Mary was the winner of Woodbury Financial's Lewis and Clark Explorer award*. This honor is awarded to a financial advisor who has demonstrated tremendous business success and growth, and provided excellent client care and service in the financial planning industry. Based on feedback she received after receiving this award, Mary created and hosted the first annual National Woodbury Women's Forum held in Dallas, TX in February 2007. Many independent female financial advisors attended the event to learn how Mary runs her practice and to discuss topics including staffing issues, acquisitions, client service, and sales. Mary now sits on the national board of Women Forward, promoting financial literacy and encouraging the growth of women in the financial industry.

Over time, Sterk Financial Services has grown, in part by acquiring five financial planning practices. Mary has become an industry specialist in the acquisition space, authoring her book, *Buy It! The Practical Guide to Buying a Financial Services Practice*. Mary does private consulting with advisors who need assistance during the acquisition process.

Mary was named one of *Wealth Magazine's* Top 50 Women in Wealth in 2008*. In 2011, Mary was given the Siouxland Women of Excellence Award for Women Taking Risks*. Following that, she was honored as one of the 2012 Top 10 Under 40 in her community*. In 2015, Mary was featured on the cover of *Siouxland Women Magazine*, as well as in the *Wall Street Journal* for her high-level estate planning*. In March of 2016 the prestigious President's Award was bestowed upon Mary by Woodbury Financial Services for long-time exemplary service and contributions to clients, community, and the financial industry.

Finally, Mary developed and has taught a class at a local college entitled "Financial Planning for Women." Mary is a member of the Siouxland Estate Planning Council, is a past Financial Services Institute board member, and the past chairperson of the Woodbury Financial Services Representative Advisory Council. Her community involvement includes being the past Chair of Women United, past President of the Western

Iowa Tech College Foundation Board, current board member of the Sioux City Art Center, and former membership as a Sioux Trails Girl Scout Leader, Siouxland Professional Women's Organization, The Greater Dakota Valley Jaycees, and staffing Premier Education's Family Values Focus seminars.

Connect with Mary at marysterk@sterkfinancialservices.com.

Third-party rankings and recognitions are no guarantee of future investment success, and do not ensure that a client or prospective client will experience a higher level of performance or results. These ratings should not be construed as an endorsement of the advisor by any client nor are they representative of any one client's evaluation. The Wealth Magazine Award was based on client assets under management and for completion of acquisitions. The Siouxland Women of Excellence Award was earned for entrepreneurial skills and achievements in creating her own company. The Top 10 Under 40 Award is bestowed on local business owners who made significant contributions of time to charitable organizations in the community.

THANK YOU

Let's Keep Talking.

Thank you for taking the time to explore your retirement journey with me, but the end of the book doesn't have to be the end of our conversation! If you would like to connect further to visit about your personal retirement planning, we would love to schedule your free Value Assessment Meeting.

During a Value Assessment Meeting, we will have a simple conversation about goals, objectives, and your hopes for the future–the starting point for any successful financial strategy. We will discuss the concerns and obstacles facing you, and help you understand the opportunities that offer you the best chance of financial success. We determine together if our firm can bring value to you, and which Certified Financial Planner™ in our office is best suited to work with your unique situation.

Based on the complexity of your plan, we will also discuss a fee for services that our office will provide for you.

We work with clients all over the United States, so near or far, we invite you to reach out to schedule your free Value Assessment Meeting.

There are three ways to schedule an appointment:

- Contact us at 605-217-3555, or toll free at 1-866-800-2186.
- Email us at Marysterk@sterkfinancialservices.com
- Schedule through our website at www.sterkfinancial services.com

Also, don't forget to download your free copy of the Strategic Retirement Tool Kit[*].

You can find it at http://www.sterkfinancialservices.com/p/toolkit

Happy retirement planning!

Securities and Investment Advisory Services are offered through Woodbury Financial Services, Inc., Member FINRA/SIPC. Insurance offered through Sterk Financial Services, which is not affiliated with Woodbury. Neither Woodbury Financial nor its representative or employees provide legal or tax advice. Sterk Financial Services is located at 350 Oak Tree Lane, Suite 150, Dakota Dunes, SD, 57049.

---

[*]   http://www.sterkfinancialservices.com/p/toolkit

A free eBook edition is available with the purchase of this book.

To claim your free eBook edition:
1. Download the Shelfie app.
2. Write your name in upper case in the box.
3. Use the Shelfie app to submit a photo.
4. Download your **eBook to any** device.

Print & Digital Together Forever.

Snap a photo

Free eBook

Read anywhere

Morgan James
Speakers Group

➤ www.TheMorganJamesSpeakersGroup.com

We connect Morgan James published
authors with live and online events
and audiences whom will benefit
from their expertise.